THE NOTEBOOK OF DOOM

ATTACK OF THE SHADOW SMASHERS

BY TROY CUMMINGS

BRANCHES™
SCHOLASTIC INC.

Read more books in THE NOTEBOOK OF DOOM series!

#1

#2

#3

#4

TABLE OF CONTENTS

To Mom:
Thanks for having me!

Thank you, Katie Carella and Liz Herzog, for your support, for your hard work, and for not throwing pine cones at me.

Library of Congress Cataloging-in-Publication Data Available

Cummings, Troy, author, illustrator.
Attack of the shadow smashers / written and illustrated by Troy Cummings.
pages cm. — (The Notebook of Doom ; 3)
Summary: The latest monsters threatening Stermont Elementary are shadowy shapeshifters that attach themselves to people, eat their shadows, and block out all light—but before he can think of a way to deal with them, Alexander has to deal with a startling revelation from his friend Nikki.

1. Monsters—Juvenile fiction. 2. Shades and shadows—Juvenile fiction.
3. Best friends—Juvenile fiction. 4. Elementary schools—Juvenile fiction.
5. Horror tales. [1. Monsters—Fiction. 2. Shadows—Fiction. 3. Best friends—Fiction.
4. Friendship—Fiction. 5. Elementary schools—Fiction. 6. Schools—Fiction. 7. Horror stories.] I. Title.
PZ7.C91494Att 2013
813.6—dc23
2013011629
ISBN: 978-93-5103-451-3

Book design by Liz Herzog

First Scholastic printing, November 2013

This reprint edition: September 2024

Printed in India

CHAPTER 1

CLEANUP CREW

The sixty-story slime creature knocked over another skyscraper.

"That's one scary monster, huh, Al?" said Alexander's dad.

Alexander Bopp yawned. “It’s a neat comic, but I wouldn’t call Swamp-Yak ‘scary.’”

“Are you nuts?!” his dad said. “He’s got seven eyes! And lightning breath!”

“Sorry, Dad,” said Alexander. “But Swamp-Yak is silly. He slips on a bowling ball and falls into a volcano — THE END. A *real* monster would be way smarter than that.”

Alexander’s dad laughed. “Oh, Al. You take this monster stuff too seriously.”

Alexander *was* serious about monsters, ever since he had moved to Stermont. The town was crawling with them. Real, scary monsters — not the kinds you find in comic books.

“All right, kiddo. You can go play outside,” said Alexander’s dad.

"Thanks, Dad!" Alexander yelled as he shot out the door and into the woods.

He followed a footpath to an old caboose. The train car was the hideout of the Super Secret Monster Patrol, which was also known as the S.S.M.P. The S.S.M.P. was a group of kids who fought monsters. This group had fallen apart years ago, but Alexander had restarted it after being attacked by monsters.

Alexander climbed into the caboose. There was stuff everywhere: papers, boxes, flashlights, ice skates, a saxophone, a birdcage, a globe, a cheese grater, and a basket of Ping-Pong balls. In other words, everything you might need to fight a monster.

In the middle of this mess sat Rip and Nikki, the only other members of the S.S.M.P.

“Sorry I’m late,” said Alexander. “How’s the cleanup going?”

“Great!” said Nikki. “I’ve been organizing all of our gear.”

“And I drew this awesome picture of me fighting balloon goons at your leap-year birthday party,” said Rip. “And look! Here’s me sword-fighting the fish-kabob monster!”

"Sheesh!" Nikki said, whipping a Ping-Pong ball at Rip. "You didn't defeat those monsters single-handed, you know."

"Fine," he said. "I'll add you to the picture. And Salamander." Salamander was Alexander's nickname. He was *almost* used to it.

"Oh, and check this out!" Rip said. He tossed something curved and white to Alexander. It was a jawbone. With fangs.

Nikki's eyes grew wide.

Alexander studied the fangs.

Rip whistled. "Those are some serious choppers! This jawbone must have come from a super-evil monster!"

"Evil?" said Nikki, sinking into her hoodie.

Alexander snapped his fingers. "I *know* this monster!" he said.

Alexander unzipped his backpack and pulled out the official S.S.M.P. notebook. He had found it on his first day in Stermont. He never went anywhere without it.

Alexander thumbed through the monster-filled pages. "I remember seeing a long-toothed monster that —"

"NO!" Nikki shouted. She tore some pages from Alexander's notebook.

Then Nikki ran out of the caboose without saying a word.

Alexander closed the notebook. "What was *that* about?" he asked.

Rip shrugged.

"AL!" shouted a voice.

"Gotta run," said Alexander. "Dad's taking me shopping for clothes."

"Oh, yeah — tomorrow's picture day," said Rip. He flexed his arms. "I should practice my poses."

Alexander shook his head.

CHAPTER 2

I SEE LONDON, I SEE FRANCE

Alexander hiked up his pants and looked in the fitting-room mirror.

I look like a rodeo clown, thought Alexander.

His dad peeked in through the curtain and smiled. "Now *those* are some snappy slacks!"

Alexander groaned. "Can't we just buy the plain black suit?"

"Sure, Al. Suit yourself!" said his dad. "I'll go pick out some ties."

Alexander closed the curtain. Then he froze. Something in the mirror had moved. A cold draft tickled his back, as if someone had forgotten to close the fridge.

"Dad?" he asked, peeking over his shoulder. "Is that you?"

The curtain was still closed.

Alexander looked back at the mirror. His eyes were bugging out. His nose was twitching. And his mustache was drooping.

Mustache? Alexander blinked. Wait . . . it was just a shadow under his nose. The shadow wiggled.

It's swaying, he thought, *like the tail of a* — he gasped — *a giant snake!*

The shadowy snake slithered across the mirror, ready to strike.

"Ack!" Alexander leaped backward, right out of his pants. And right out of the fitting room. He crashed into a rack of belts.

"I found a tie," said Alexander's dad, strolling into view. He lowered an eyebrow.

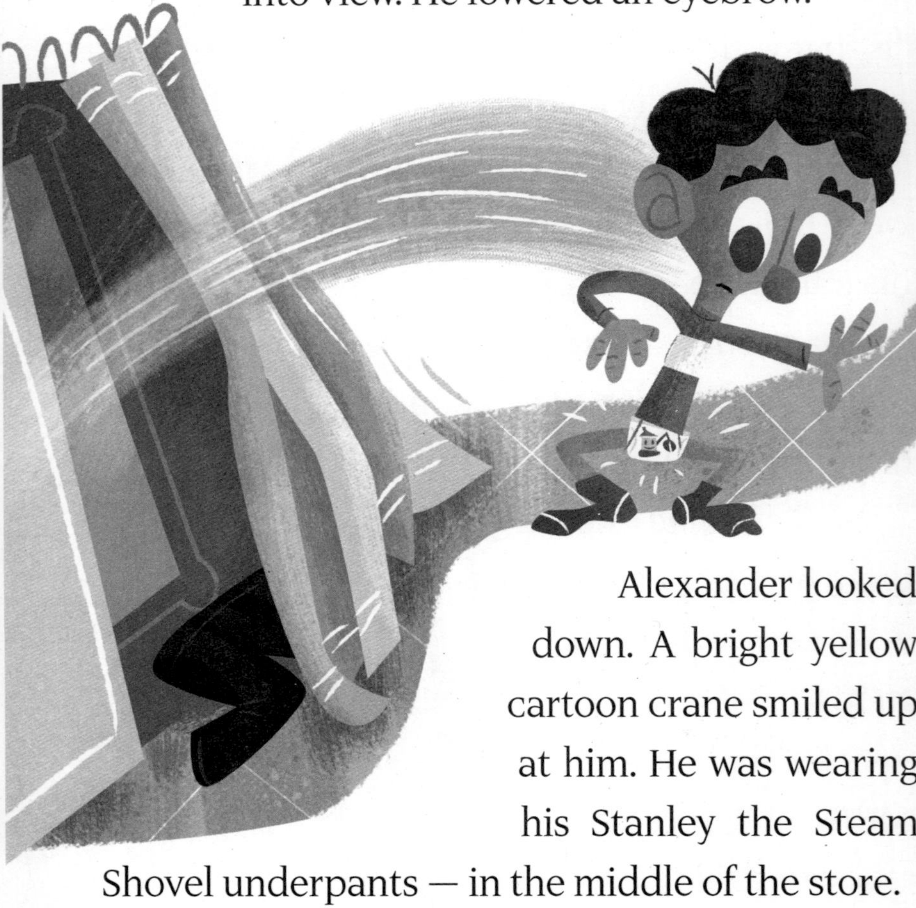

Alexander looked down. A bright yellow cartoon crane smiled up at him. He was wearing his Stanley the Steam Shovel underpants — in the middle of the store.

Alexander's knees wobbled. "I, um . . ."

His dad chuckled as he pulled open the fitting-room curtain. "Let's get you back into your big-boy pants."

Alexander slowly stepped back inside. There was no sign of the snake shadow.

Did I see a monster? Alexander wondered. *Or was that snake-thing just a trick of the light?*

Alexander got dressed and followed his dad to the checkout counter. "Snakes . . . eels . . . a leech, maybe?" He muttered to himself as he flipped through the monster notebook.

SCREECH LEECH

A long purple three-eyed leech.

HABITAT

Found in closets. (They blend in with the belts and neckties.)

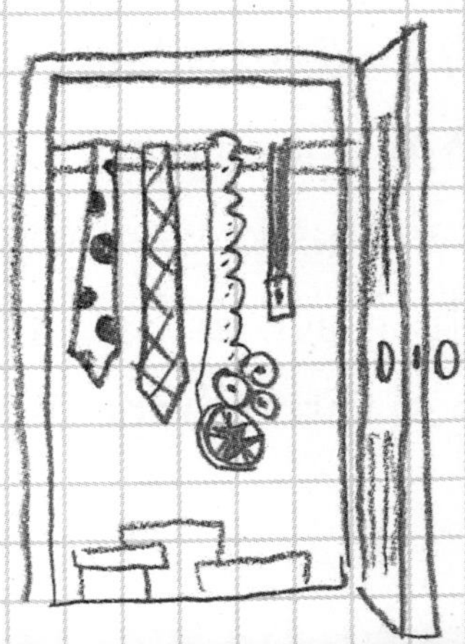

A screech leech's cry sounds like a duck playing a broken kazoo.

DIET Chipmunks. Preferably with BBQ sauce.

BEHAVIOR These bloodsuckers scream when they're hungry.

WARNING! When you're near a closet, NEVER act like a chipmunk!

Alexander closed the notebook.

Could that thing in the fitting room have been a screech leech? he thought. *I'll have to see what Rip and Nikki think tomorrow at school.*

CHAPTER 3

PHOTO NO-NO

Alexander fiddled with his tie as he hurried to the old hospital. Actually, it wasn't a hospital. It was where he went to school while the new Stermont Elementary building was being built. But today, as he stepped inside, he saw that it wasn't a hospital *or* a school. It was a cornfield.

A fake cornfield. There was a fake wooden fence, a fake wagon wheel, and a row of fake corn with a beautiful fake sunset.

There was even a fake scarecrow behind the camera. Wait. It wasn't a scarecrow: It was Mr. Hoarsely. To most kids, he was the school secretary, but Alexander, Rip, and Nikki knew him as a member of the original S.S.M.P.

"Alexander, you're late!" said Mr. Hoarsely.

Alexander's classmates were lined up behind the wagon wheel. Alexander wondered how long they'd been holding their poses.

"Uh, sorry," Alexander said. He took a spot between Rip and Nikki.

"About time, Salamander!" said Rip. He wore a clip-on tie, and it looked like someone had even tried to comb his hair this morning.

"Quiet down, please!" said Mr. Hoarsely.

"Guys," Alexander whispered, "I saw a monster yesterday!"

"Really? Cool!" said Rip.

"Oh," said Nikki. She hadn't dressed up for picture day.

"Um, Nikki?" said Alexander. "Is something wrong?"

Nikki pulled her hood down to her eyebrows. "I'm just not big on photos," she said.

"I hear you," said Rip. "It must be hard to be in a picture with a good-looking guy like me."

Nikki groaned.

"Smile, everyone," said Mr. Hoarsely.

Everyone smiled. Actually, not quite everyone.

"You, too, Nikki," said Mr. Hoarsely.

Nikki didn't smile.

Mr. Hoarsely sighed. "Maybe you could — *eep!*" He tripped on his tripod as a mean-looking woman pushed her way through the corn.

It was Principal Vanderpants.

"Nikki," she said. "Would you be so kind as to smile for one hundredth of a second, so Mr. Hoarsely can photograph your class?"

Nikki tightened her lips. She looked like she had swallowed a bug.

"No good," said Ms. Vanderpants, shaking her head. "Smile, Nikki!"

Nikki bared her teeth. Her smile was wide and bright. But two of her teeth were extra long. And pointy.

A second later, she snapped her mouth shut.

Alexander blinked.

CHAPTER 4 RED IN THE FACE

"Rip! We *have* to talk!" said Alexander.

He ran to the lunch line, where Rip was getting a tray.

"Hey," said Rip. "Look! For once, I am not grossed out by lunch. Although I can't say I'm thrilled about the rest of the week."

"Forget the menu!" said Alexander. "Have you noticed anything strange . . . about Nikki?"

Rip took a plate of chicken fingers. "Like how she ripped those pages from the notebook yesterday?"

"No, not that," said Alexander. "Well, maybe that." He spoke quietly. "Nikki has *fangs*, Rip."

"Oh, geez!" said Rip, grinning. "There's no way Nikki's got fangs."

Alexander frowned. "But I saw —"

"Hey, guys," said Nikki, stepping in between them. "I saved us a spot."

Alexander followed Rip and Nikki to a table.

"So, Salamander," said Nikki. She punched a straw into a juice box. "Tell us about this monster you saw yesterday."

Alexander hadn't noticed it before, but Nikki barely moved her lips when she talked. He couldn't get a good look at her teeth.

"Well," he said. "I was trying on pants, when —"

"GROSS!" Rip yelled, pointing his chicken finger at Nikki. "What are you doing?"

BLOOP! BLOP!

Nikki was pouring tons of ketchup all over her plate.

"What?" she asked.

Rip made a face. "I was hoping to make it through lunch without gagging."

Nikki drowned a tiny nugget of chicken in her lake of ketchup. Then she ate it. A drop of red rolled down her chin.

Alexander stared at Nikki. "So . . . anyway. Maybe it was just a shadow, but I think I saw a snake monster. Or a leech."

"A leech?!" said Rip. "Bloodsucking monsters are the *worst*! With their fangs and —"

"ENOUGH!" Nikki shouted. She grabbed her juice box and — **SPLISSHH!** — sprayed Rip in the face. Then she stomped out of the cafeteria.

"What did I say?" asked Rip, dripping with cherry punch.

Alexander handed Rip a napkin. "I'm not sure," he said. "But you should probably wash up."

Rip headed to the bathroom. As Alexander nibbled a chicken finger, he noticed a strange shadow along one wall. It was shaped like a sledgehammer.

The hammer shadow rose up as Rip walked by and then it silently smashed down — right onto Rip's own shadow.

Rip shivered a moment, but kept walking.

Alexander stopped chewing.

Rip's shadow had sprouted antlers!

CHAPTER

5 OPEN WIDE

During math class, Alexander checked the monster notebook. He found nothing about creepy animal-shaped shadows.

BRINNGGG!

As the final bell rang, Alexander hurried over to Rip's desk.

"What's up, Salamander?" Rip asked. "Does Nikki have tentacles now?"

"No!" said Alexander. "It's your shadow! It's turned into some kind of reindeer creature."

"What?" Rip said. He glanced at the wall. Rip's shadow was back to normal: no antlers.

He looked back at Alexander and cleared his throat. "Ahem."

"I don't understand!" said Alexander. "Your shadow was all wonky at lunch!"

Rip laughed. "Hey, Nikki!" he called. "Help me talk some sense into — Oh. She's gone already."

Alexander slouched. "Never mind, Rip. I should go, too. I'm meeting Dad at his office."

"All right," Rip said. "Watch for reindeer!"

Alexander's dad's office was only a few blocks from school, but the walk there felt like 100 miles.

I've only made two friends since moving here, thought Alexander, *and now they've got fangs and antlers! Am I going bananas?*

"Hello, kiddo," called a voice.

Alexander stopped at a sign reading BOPP DENTISTRY. His dad was kneeling behind the sign.

"My poor tulips," he said. "It's like they're not getting enough sunlight."

"Maybe they're being blocked by —" Alexander shuddered. A chill crept up his back. He saw his father's shadow stretch across the lawn. It was shaped like a T. rex.

"Dad! Your shadow!" Alexander yelled. "It's a dinosaur!"

As Alexander's dad stood up, his dino shadow twisted back into a regular people shadow.

"Oh, Al," he said. "It's just the light. Haven't you seen a shadow puppet before?" He wove his fingers together. "Look! A birdie!"

"I don't know, Dad," said Alexander. "Your shadow looked —" His eyes grew huge. "Nikki? What are *you* doing here?"

Nikki came up the walk. "Oh, hi, Salamander," she said. "I'm here to see your dad."

"Howdy!" said Alexander's dad.

Nikki swallowed. "Uh, hi, Mr. Bopp. I was hoping you could help me with" — she shot Alexander a glance — "my teeth."

"Anything for a pal of Al's!" said Alexander's dad. "What exactly is the problem?"

Nikki closed her eyes and then opened her mouth wide.

Alexander's dad leaned in for a look. "Those are some serious choppers!" he said.

He turned back to Alexander. "Son, why don't you run home and start on your homework?"

"Ugh," said Alexander.

"Meanwhile, Nikki and I will head inside and see what we can do about her overbite."

He said "overbite," and not "fangs"! Maybe Nikki is normal after all, thought Alexander. *Not like that dino shadow!*

CHAPTER 6

IN THE DARK

"Good morning, early bird!" sang a chirpy voice. Alexander's teacher popped out of a hatch in the classroom wall.

Alexander sighed. "Hi, Mr. Plunkett."

"You're just in time to help," Mr. Plunkett said. He wheeled out an old machine that looked like a cross between a telescope and a toaster. "You'll be running the projector today."

Alexander fussed with the projector while the rest of the class arrived. Rip gave Alexander a slap on the back as he walked by. Alexander noticed Rip's shadow was Rip-shaped.

Then Nikki showed up. At least, she *looked* like Nikki. But she *seemed* like a totally different girl. She took long steps. She held her head high. And then, she smiled. It was a mile-wide, eyes-closed, stretch-your-cheeks kind of smile.

"Salamander!" Nikki stepped in front of the projector's beam. Alexander squinted as light reflected off the silver wires on her teeth. "I love love *love* my new braces!" she said. "Your dad's the best!"

Her teeth seemed less pointy with the braces. *How could I have thought she was a monster?* thought Alexander. Then he gasped.

Although Nikki stood directly in the light, she had no shadow!

FLICK! Out went the lights. "Okay, class," Mr. Plunkett said. "What's special about tomorrow?"

"It's Gopher Day!" shouted everyone except Alexander.

Gopher Day? Alexander wondered.

"Yes, Gopher Day!" said Mr. Plunkett. "So instead of a boring old science lesson, we're going to watch a filmstrip today!"

Everyone cheered. Except Alexander, again.

"Mr. Bopp, start the film!"

EVERY YEAR AT NOON
ON THE FIRST DAY
OF SPRING . . .
EVERYONE IN
STERMONT GOES
TO DERWOOD PARK . . .
TO SEE THE STAR OF GOPHER DAY:
STERMONT STELLA!

Suddenly, a dark blur washed across the screen.

"Boooo!" the class shouted.

Alexander fiddled with some knobs, but the smudge wouldn't budge.

"Aw, nuts — show's over, folks!" said Mr. Plunkett, switching the lights back on. "Remember: Bring your families to Gopher Day!"

"And also," said Mr. Plunkett, waving a large envelope, "your pictures are ready." He handed out the photos.

Alexander stared at the class picture, wide-eyed. Right there, looming behind his classmates, were the monsters he'd been looking for.

CHAPTER 7

THE OTHER MONSTER

Alexander sat alone on the low end of the teeter-totter. He took the folded note from his pocket and reread it.

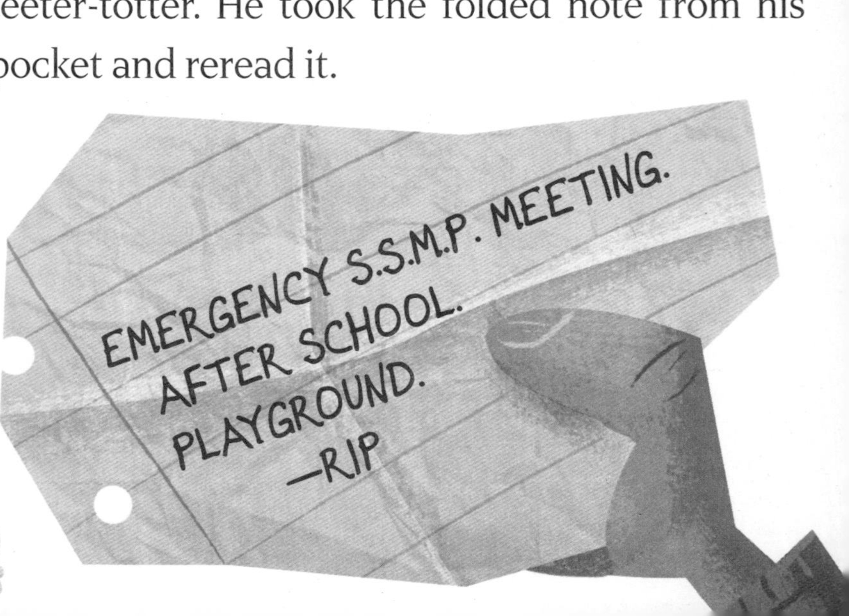

Suddenly:

"Whoa!" Alexander found himself teetering three feet in the air. Rip had jumped onto the totter end.

"Okay, weenie," Rip said. "You were right about the shadow monsters."

Alexander held up the class photo. "They really ruined our picture, didn't they?"

"Picture, shmicture!" said Rip. "I'm talking about *me*! I got in trouble last night for staying up late. But I didn't do it!"

Rip took a step back. Alexander crashed to the ground.

"It was after bedtime," said Rip. "Mom was taking out the trash, and she thought she saw me through the curtains, dancing around — wearing antlers."

"You were dancing?" asked Alexander.

"No! I was asleep!" Rip barked. "My stupid reindeer shadow was dancing! But when Mom flipped on the light to yell at me, it was gone!"

Rip looked at Alexander. Alexander did not know what to say.

"So when did that shadow thing get me, anyhow?" asked Rip.

"Yesterday, after lunch," said Alexander. "The shadow smashed onto you when you were walking to the bathroom. And I have already checked the notebook — there's nothing about them in there."

"Hmm . . ." said Rip.

"Hey, guys!" Nikki trotted over. "*There* you are!"

Alexander smiled. "Nikki!"

"So get this, Nikki," said Rip. "Stermont is swarming with shadow smashers!"

"Oh, really . . ." said Nikki, jamming her hands into her hoodie pocket.

"Yeah!" said Alexander, "I've seen them all over town: in the fitting room, in our class photo, on my dad, and, um, on Rip. They even screwed up the Gopher Day filmstrip and my dad's tulips. We should —"

"Stop," said Nikki.

Alexander and Rip gave Nikki a puzzled look.

"We need to talk about *another* monster in Stermont," she said.

"Ugh," said Rip. "You mean we have to fight something *besides* shadow smashers?"

"I hope not," said Nikki. She looked at Alexander as she pulled the torn-out notebook pages from her pocket. "The other monster is *me*."

CHAPTER

8 FANGS FOR THE MEMORIES

"Umm . . ." Alexander was speechless.

"Poor Nikki," said Rip, shaking his head. "Sure, you're a weirdo. But a *monster*?!"

Nikki handed over the notebook pages. Alexander and Rip looked at the drawings and then at Nikki.

"This . . . is you?" asked Rip.

"Sort of," said Nikki. "But the entry was all wrong, so I fixed it." She took a roll of tape from her pocket. "Here, I'll put these pages back."

JAMPIRE

A ~~terrible undead monster~~.

smart, brave girl.

HABITAT ~~Graveyards.~~

Grade schools!

PEEK! Jampires have no shadows.

Yuck! No!

DIET ~~Blood?~~ Anything red and juicy: ketchup, fruit punch, raspberry jam, jelly donuts, strawberry gummies.

BEHAVIOR Jampires are ~~evil~~. friendly.

Also, they can see in the dark.

WARNING!

Keep jampires out of direct sunlight!

"So. Any questions about jampires?" said Nikki. "I'll tell you anything. But you've got to promise to keep my secret!"

"Cross my heart," said Alexander.

"And hope to die!" said Rip. He frowned. "No, wait. Hope to sprain my ankle!"

"Good enough," said Nikki.

"Okay," said Alexander. "Can you turn into a bat?"

Nikki rolled her eyes. "No. That's ridiculous."

"Or eat people's brains?" added Rip.

"Gross, no!" said Nikki. "It's mostly a lot of little things: like seeing in the dark, or getting sunburns in like five seconds."

"Or casting no shadow during the filmstrip," said Alexander. "You really are a . . . uh . . ."

"A monster," Rip mumbled.

"I wasn't going to tell you," said Nikki, "but then I lost my baby teeth and my fangs started coming in. So I thought I should be honest with . . . you know, my best friends."

Again, Alexander was speechless.

But not Rip. "Thanks," he said, "for lying to us this whole time."

Nikki took a step back. "I didn't — I would *never* lie to you! I just —"

She rushed off the playground.

"Rip! Go easy on her!" said Alexander. "It was brave of Nikki to tell us her secret."

"Yeah," said Rip. "So when are you going to kick her out of the S.S.M.P.?"

Alexander's jaw dropped. "Huh?"

"We can't have a *monster* in the Super Secret *Monster* Patrol!" Rip said. "She's what we are supposed to be fighting!"

Alexander looked at Rip.

"It's your call, Salamander. You're the head of the club," said Rip.

"Um, can we talk about this tomorrow?" Alexander said.

"Fine," said Rip. "Let's meet at the caboose in the morning, since there's no school. What are you doing tonight, anyway?"

"It's board game night," said Alexander. "I should go."

CHAPTER 9

BRIGHT IDEA

"Help!" Alexander's dad shouted. "I'm being swallowed by a nine-armed space-blob!"

"Okay, Dad," said Alexander. He rolled a six and saved his dad.

Alexander's dad looked up from his cards. "Something tells me you're not into this game."

Alexander dumped his spaceships back in the box. “Sorry, Dad. It’s been a rough day.”

“Cheer up, Al,” his dad said. “Tomorrow’s Gopher Day!”

“Yeah,” said Alexander. He gave his dad a hug and shuffled up to bed.

Alexander read the notebook for a while before finally turning off his flashlight. His bedroom went dark.

Maybe Rip's right. Maybe we should *kick Nikki out of the S.S.M.P.*, he thought. *But we're a team.*

He let out a long sigh. Then he gasped — he could see his breath! The room had suddenly become icy cold — just like that time in the fitting room.

A shadow smasher! He jolted upright. The dark shadow glided across a patch of moonlight on the wall. Straight for his bed.

Alexander rolled to the floor. The shadow twisted into a sledgehammer, and — **POW!**

Alexander's feet felt all tingly. He looked back and saw that his shadow had grown into the shape of a giant spider.

The spider shadow followed him along a wall. Alexander scrambled toward the opposite corner of his room. **CONK!** — he bumped his night-light.

Suddenly, the spider shadow paused, all eight legs trembling.

Is it afraid of me? Alexander wondered, sitting up. *No, not me — it's the light! Just like how Rip's reindeer shadow disappeared when his mom turned on his bedroom light!*

Alexander kicked his nightstand. His flashlight fell off, rolling toward him. He pointed it at the shadow smasher and flicked the switch.

The spider shadow quivered in the light. Then it peeled away from Alexander's feet and dashed under the bed.

Alexander quickly dragged a lamp and a glow-in-the-dark sword over to the night-light. He made a circle of light and sat in the middle, on a nest made of blankets.

"Sorry, shadow smasher," Alexander said to the underside of his bed. "Looks like I'll be reading 'til sunrise." He opened the S.S.M.P. notebook.

CHAPTER 10

TOTALLY FLOORED

Alexander woke up on the floor. His room was warm with sunlight, and there was no sign of the shadow smasher.

His now-dead flashlight lay near the open notebook. . . .

SOCKTOPUS

A woven monster
with eight mismatched arms.

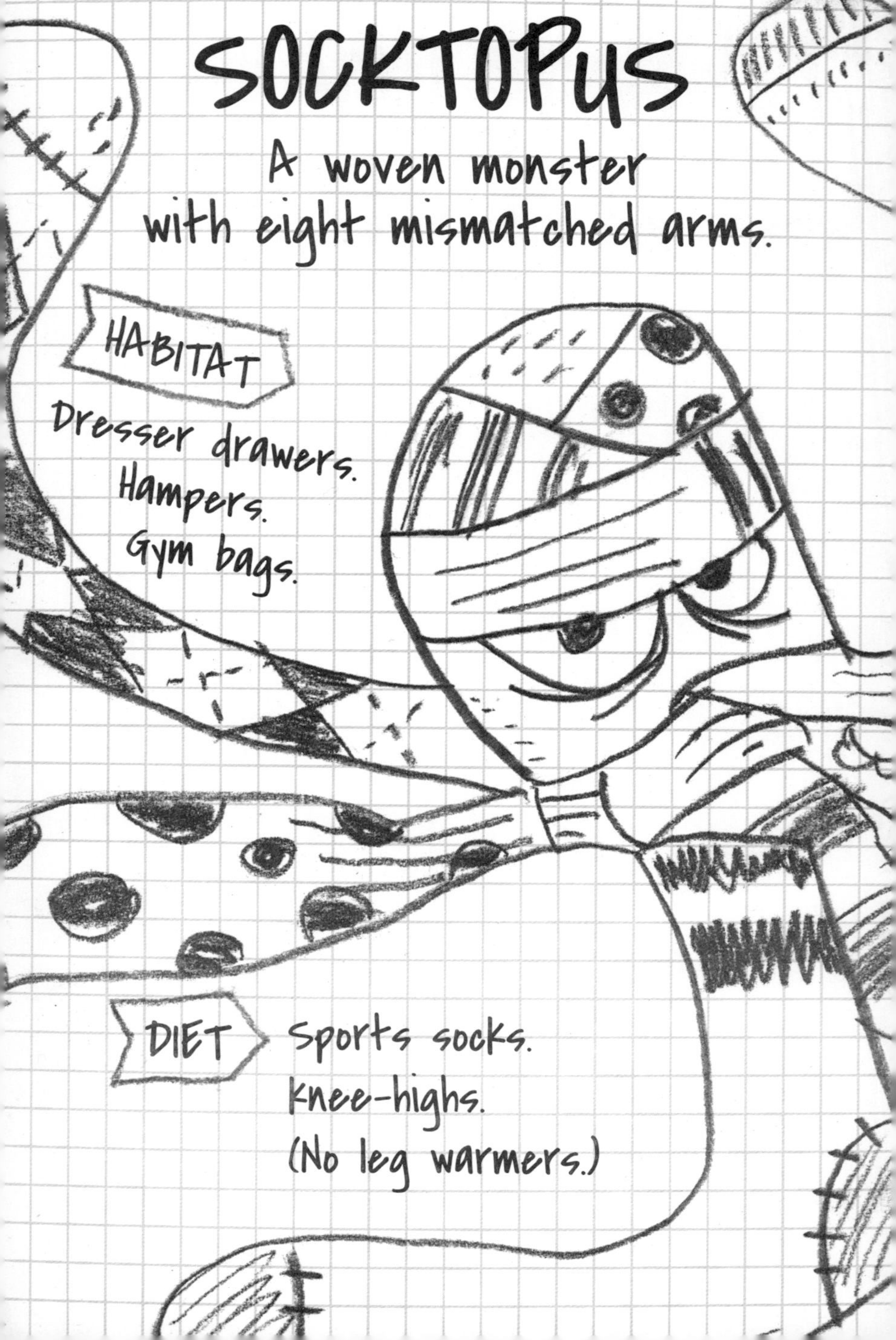

HABITAT

Dresser drawers.
Hampers.
Gym bags.

DIET

Sports socks.
Knee-highs.
(No leg warmers.)

PEE-YEW! The stench of an unwashed socktopus can out-stink a skunk.

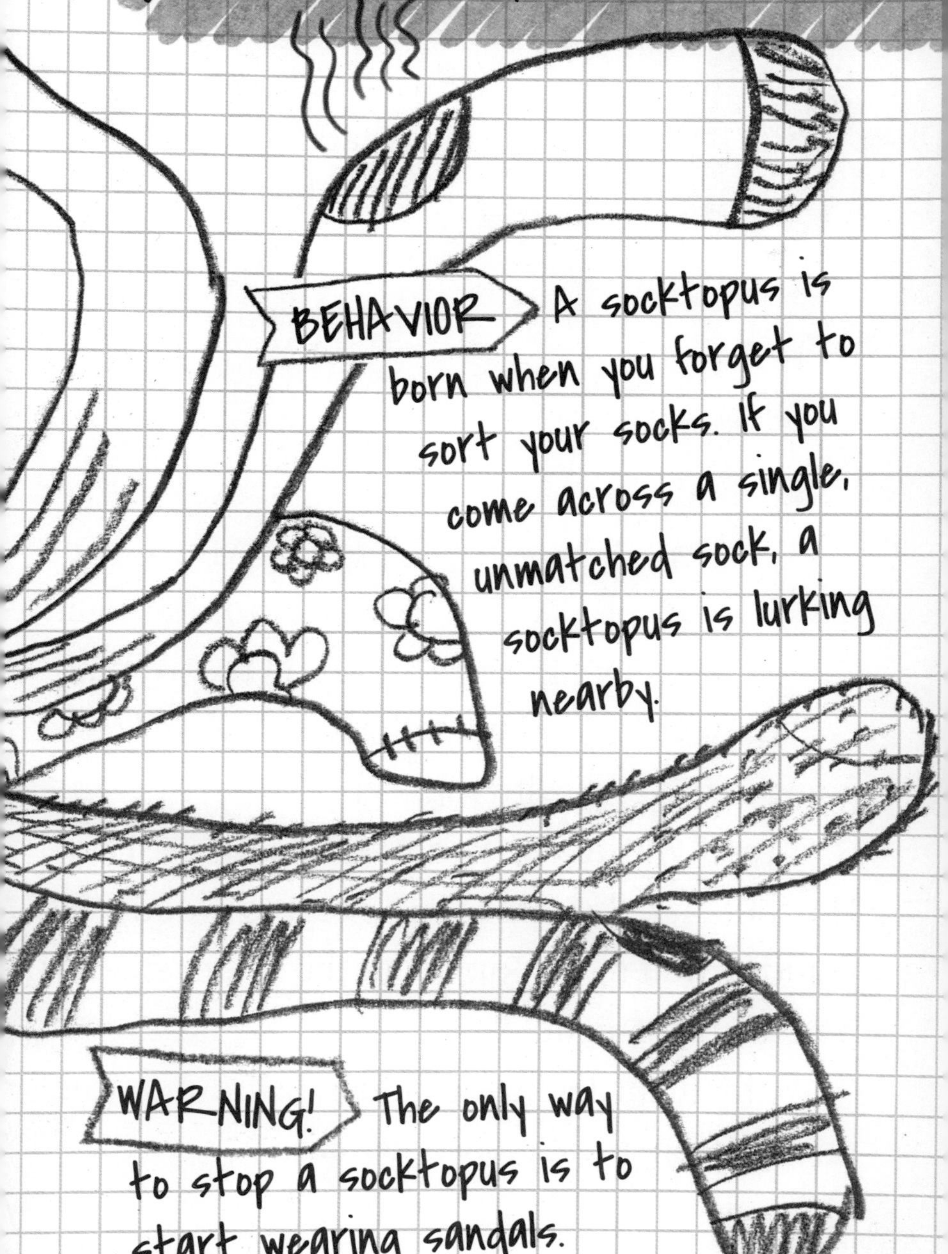

BEHAVIOR A socktopus is born when you forget to sort your socks. If you come across a single, unmatched sock, a socktopus is lurking nearby.

WARNING! The only way to stop a socktopus is to start wearing sandals.

Alexander closed the notebook and sat up. His shadow sat up, too.

"You're just my regular shadow, right?" said Alexander.

He did a little chicken dance. His shadow copied his funky moves exactly.

Alexander ran downstairs and gobbled up his breakfast in record time.

"Happy Gopher Day, Al!" his dad said. "You're going to the park with Rip, right?"

"Yep!" Alexander said. "See you there, Dad!" He shot out the door and into the woods. He couldn't wait to tell Rip about the spider shadow and the night-light.

A moment later, Alexander heard a scream coming from the caboose. **ARRGH!**

CHAPTER 11

SHADOW BOXING

Rip!" Alexander called, racing into the caboose. "What's going on?"

Rip was sitting on an overturned crate, rubbing his knuckles.

"Here's a tip, Salamander," Rip growled. "Don't try to punch your shadow."

Alexander spotted a fist-size dent in the wall. "Wait," he said, "why would you punch —"

"The shadow smashers got me, okay?!" Rip said, pointing to the floor. "Look!"

Rip now had the shadow of a very large, very cute, fluffy bunny.

Alexander tried not to smile.

"What a weenie shadow!" Rip yelled. "The reindeer was better."

Rip sat back, crossing his arms. His bunny shadow wiggled its ears.

"So how do we get rid of these things?"

"I'll show you," Alexander said.

He grabbed a flashlight from the shelf and aimed it at Rip's heels. **CLICK!** Alexander blasted the bunny with light. The bunny shadow's whiskers twitched.

Then the bunny shadow peeled itself away from Rip's feet. It was trapped between the flashlight and a sunbeam.

Alexander tossed the flashlight to Rip. "All right, bunny," he said. "Tell us your evil plan, or my friend here will zap you with the light."

The shadow smasher shrugged.

"Okay," said Alexander. "Why do you smash people's shadows?"

The bunny made nibbling motions.

"You eat shadows?"

The bunny nodded.

"You're eating *my* shadow?!" Rip yelled.

The bunny shook its head.

"You're *not* eating his shadow?" asked Alexander. "Why not?"

The bunny marched in place.

"To walk?" Alexander rubbed his chin. "You're attaching to Rip so you can go somewhere?"

The bunny nodded.

"Are all of you shadow smashers going to the same place? Somewhere in Stermont?"

The bunny nodded. Then it twisted itself into the shape of a tree.

"You're all coming here, to these woods?" guessed Alexander.

"No — to Derwood Park!" Rip shouted. "The shadow smashers must want to wreck Gopher Day! Everyone will be there!"

The bunny nodded.

Rip checked a clock on the caboose's wall. "Gopher Day starts at noon! That's in twenty minutes! We've got to get over there!"

Even though it was a sunny day, Alexander grabbed every flashlight he could find.

"Hang on!" said Rip. "What are we going to do about Nikki?"

"That will have to wait," Alexander said. "Stermont needs us!"

The boys shot out of the caboose, leaving the bunny in their dust.

CHAPTER

12 GOPHER DAY!

Derwood Park was packed with balloons, snacks, and people.

"Wow! Gopher Day is a *big* deal," said Alexander.

"I know," Rip said. "The whole town shuts down for this thing. If you ask me —" He looked back at Alexander, who had stopped in the middle of the crowd. "What?" he asked.

"Look," Alexander said, nodding toward the sidewalk.

Rip looked down. The people walking by were casting strange shadows. Some had horns, some had wings, some had tentacles. But none of the shadows looked human.

"It's crazy how nobody seems upset by their weird shadows," said Alexander.

"But wait! Look over there!" said Rip. "That kid with the camel shadow is going nuts!"

The boy was trying to point out a shadow smasher to his mom. She didn't seem interested, even when the camel shadow did a handstand.

Just then, two shoes stepped into view — with no shadow.

"Nikki!" said Alexander, looking up. He glanced at Rip, who glared back.

"I'm glad I found you guys," said Nikki.

"Not *now*!" Rip shouted. "One monster at a time! We'll handle the shadow smashers, and *then* we'll kick you out — I mean we'll talk — I mean . . . um . . . Salamander?"

Nikki looked at Alexander. "What's he talking about?"

Alexander sighed. "Nikki, we feel awful about this, but as members of the Super Secret *Monster* Patrol, we have, I guess, a duty to . . . That is . . ."

"Wait!" Nikki laughed. "Are you kicking me out of the S.S.M.P.?"

"Um," said Alexander. "I, uh . . ."

"Well, that's just perfect," said Nikki. "Because I actually came by to tell you I QUIT!"

The boys' mouths fell open.

"Oh, please!" said Nikki. "The S.S.M.P. fights monsters! Monsters like, oh, I don't know . . . ME! I don't want to be in your stupid monster-hating club anyway!"

Alexander frowned. "But —"

"Yeah, yeah," Rip said. "It's a real stake through the heart. Now let's *go*, Salamander!"

"Well, good!" said Nikki. She spun on her heels and disappeared into the crowd.

Before Alexander could say anything, he felt a jerk at his arm. "It's almost noon," said Rip, "and I think I know where the shadow smashers will strike!"

CHAPTER 13

THE HOLE STORY

Alexander and Rip squeezed through the balloon-holding, song-singing, pretzel-eating crowd of people with strange shadows. The boys soon found themselves near a bandstand.

A brass band honked its way through "You Are My Sunshine." The bandleader had a familiar shock of white hair.

"It's Mr. Hoarsely!" said Alexander.

"Never mind him," said Rip. "Check out the gopher hole."

There was a sign in front of the bandstand:

The sign pointed to a hole in the ground.

"Now everyone is just waiting for Stella to pop out," said Rip. "If she doesn't see her shadow, it means we'll have an awesome spring."

"Gopher Day sounds just like Groundhog Day," said Alexander.

"What? NO!" Rip shouted. "Oh, wait. Maybe."

Rip leaned in and whispered. "But I think Gopher Day is totally rigged! She *never* sees her shadow!"

The band played a loud "TA-DAAA!"

"Here we go!" said Rip.

Alexander scanned the crowd. The shadow smashers were pulling away from everyone's feet. They hopped from shadow to shadow until they reached the edges of the park.

Everyone's shadows were back to normal.

"I don't get it," said Rip. "Why did the shadow smashers all leave?"

The crowd grew silent as Stella peeped out of her hole. She ran into the open. Then she sat on the ground and scratched her ear.

The audience cheered.

"Hooray!" said a man in a gopher hat. "Stella didn't see her shadow! Sunny days are on the way!"

Just then, the air grew as cold as winter. From all corners of the park, shadow smashers melted together and stretched upward, totally blocking out the sun. The daytime sky became entirely dark — like the darkest night, with no stars.

Alexander could see his breath as he spoke. “We’re too late. The shadow smashers have made a shadow dome over Stermont!”

Stella squeaked as she looked up at the darkened sky. Then she scampered back into her hole.

CHAPTER

14 SKY'S THE LIMIT

Despite the totally dark sky at noon on the first day of spring, the adults in the crowd were chatting happily. The kids, however, were starting to lose it.

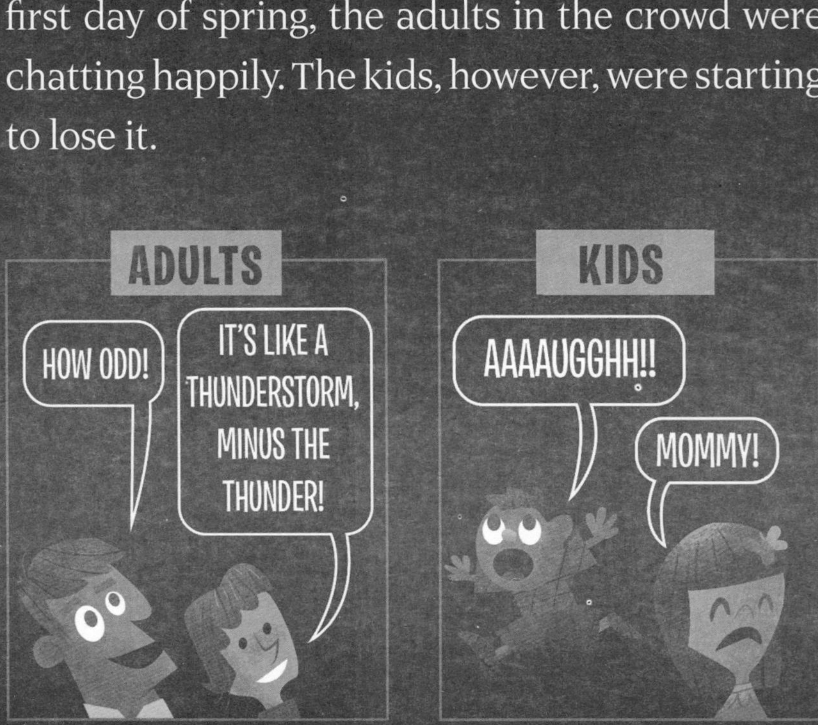

"What's with these grown-ups?" Alexander asked. "It's like they don't see what's going on. Except for Mr. Hoarsely."

The boys watched as he dove behind a huge spotlight near the bandstand.

"It's getting even darker!" said Rip. "I can't see the edge of the park!"

Alexander gave Rip a couple of flashlights. "Let's try to light up the sky!"

The boys ran around, waving their flashlights at the shadow dome.

The sky began to grumble.

"Is it working?" asked Rip.

"I'm not sure," said Alexander, "Maybe we could —"

"Hey, Al!" chirped a voice. Alexander's dad jumped out from the darkness. "Boy, Gopher Day is — hey, are you playing flashlight tag?"

Alexander glanced at Rip. "Uh, actually, Dad —"

"Swell!" said Alexander's dad. "Here, give me a flashlight." He closed his eyes and began counting to 100.

Rip and Alexander both rolled their eyes.

"Okay, Rip," said Alexander, "let's aim for the exact same spot."

Rip pointed his flashlight straight up. Alexander angled his to match.

This time, the sky grumbled much louder.

"GIVE UP!"

A loud voice thundered from the sky.

Alone, the shadow smashers had been silent. But together, they spoke in a booming voice.

"WE HAVE ALL COME TOGETHER TO BLANKET STERMONT IN ETERNAL DARKNESS!"

The rumbling grew louder yet, and the sky became even darker. Now the flashlights only seemed to shine a few feet in front of them.

"It's no use," said Rip. "Our lights are too weak."

"IT WILL ALWAYS BE PAST YOUR BEDTIME! AND STERMONT WILL BE OURS!"

"All right, we get it, shadow smashers," growled Rip. "You're scary monsters who want us gone."

"STERMONT WILL BE DARK AND WINTERY ALL YEAR LONG! NO TREES! NO FLOWERS! AND CERTAINLY NO PEOPLE!"

Alexander lowered his flashlight. "The two of us are no match for a gazillion shadow smashers."

Then he felt a tap on his shoulder. "No, but the *three* of us might be."

Nikki stepped out of the gloom.

"Nikki!" said Alexander. "You came back?"

Even Rip seemed happy to see her.

"Yep," said Nikki, flipping her hood off her head. "I took an oath to protect my town, and I intend to keep it. Now all we need is a plan!"

CHAPTER 15 A TIGHT SPOT

Since moving to Stermont, Alexander had been yelled at by bullies, teachers, and monsters. But getting yelled at by the sky was another thing altogether.

"FEAR US, SUN LOVERS! WE ARE NOW ONE POWERFUL SHADOW!"

Alexander's eyes brightened. "That's it!"

He whispered to his friends. A moment later, the three of them split up.

It was getting darker by the second. Alexander could no longer see his feet. He carefully made his way over to the gopher hole.

"Hey, smashers!" Alexander shouted, waving to the sky. "A little bunny told me you love to snack on shadows . . . especially bold, juicy shadows like mine! Check it out!"

CLUNK!

Rip switched on the spotlight, bathing Alexander in white light. His long, dark shadow cut across the park.

KA-BLASH!

There was a peal of thunder as the shadow smashers in the sky licked their chops.

“TURN OFF THAT LIGHT!!”

They all barreled down toward Alexander.

CHAPTER

16 SPRING IN HER STEP

"Now!" shouted Alexander.

He dove out of the way as Nikki sprang from behind the bandstand. She quickly took his place near the gopher hole. Rip held the spotlight steady, shining the light directly onto Nikki. Even standing in the powerful spotlight's beam, she cast no shadow. Nikki closed her eyes and gritted her teeth.

The first shadow smashed onto the ground behind her, fixing itself to her heels.

It looked over at Alexander and blinked.

GORAARRRGHH!!

With a terrible moan, a gazillion more shadow missiles rained down on that exact spot. Nikki didn't move. Over and over, the shadows smashed against one another, becoming darker and blurrier.

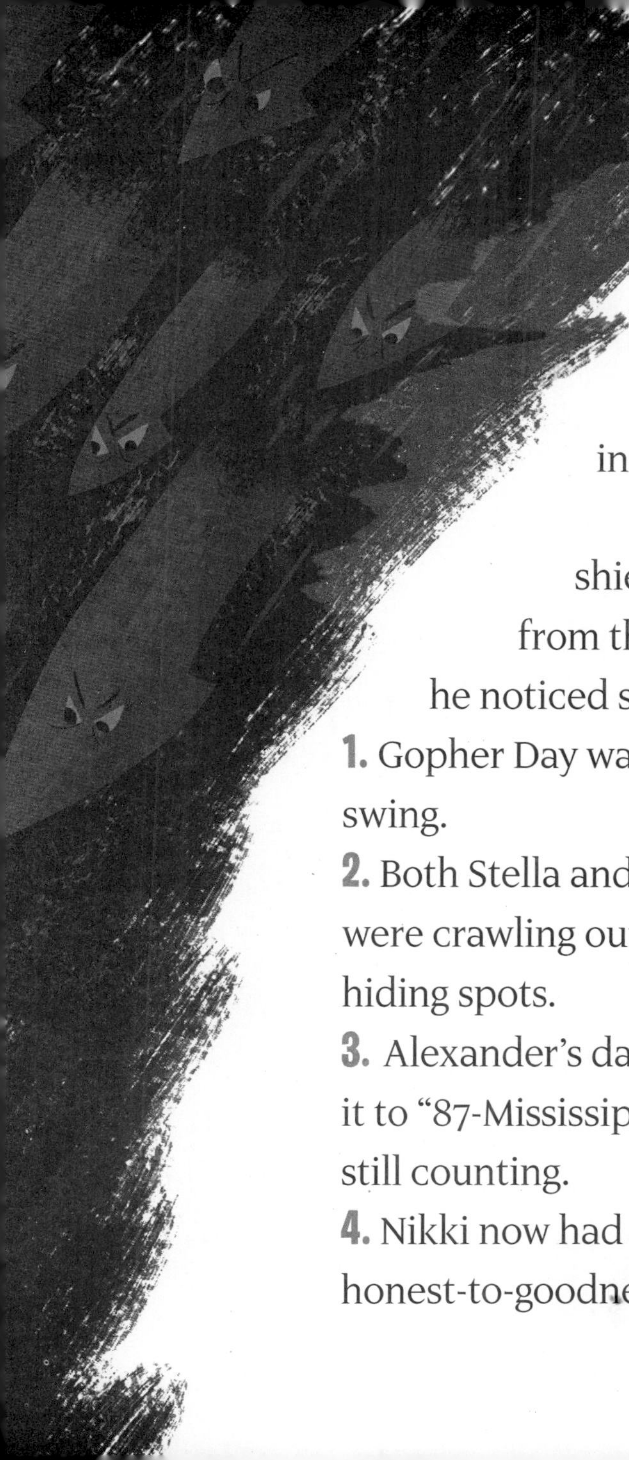

The sky
became
instantly sunny.
As Alexander
shielded his eyes
from the brightness,
he noticed several things:

1. Gopher Day was back in full swing.
2. Both Stella and Mr. Hoarsely were crawling out of their hiding spots.
3. Alexander's dad had made it to "87-Mississippi," and was still counting.
4. Nikki now had her own honest-to-goodness shadow.

"This is so cool," said Nikki. She skipped around, watching her new shadow move with her. "Did it work? Are they really trapped?"

"Well, that first shadow smasher looked confused when it got stuck to your heels, since you had no shadow for it to take over. Then the rest of them did what they do best: smash!" said Alexander. "By the time they all smashed together, they must've flattened themselves into one plain old shadow. Or something."

Rip ran over and offered a fist bump. "Nikki!" he hollered. "You rule!" He turned to Alexander. "I can't believe you wanted to kick her out of the S.S.M.P.!"

Alexander fake-punched Rip's arm.

"You know," said Alexander. "We three are running the show now, so we get to make up some new rules from time to time!" He flipped open the notebook and wrote on the inside cover:

RULE #1: NOT ALL MONSTERS ARE BAD.

Alexander smiled at Nikki. "Rip and I may not be jampires, and you may not be human, but who cares?! What matters is that we stick together. Nikki, will you please rejoin the Super Secret Monster Patrol?"

Nikki looked a little sunburned. Or maybe she was blushing.

"Of course I will," she said. "But first, add the shadow smashers to the notebook!"

SHADOW SMASHER

A shady shape-shifter. Shadow smashers hate light and will block it whenever possible. This is bad news for:

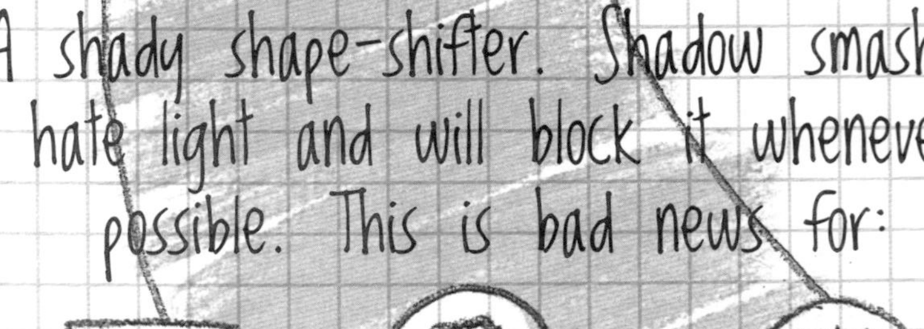

BRRRR! Shadow smashers bring a chill to the air.

HABITAT Right behind you.

DIET They "attach" to people and slowly eat their shadows.

BEHAVIOR Shadow smashers travel by jumping from shadow to shadow.

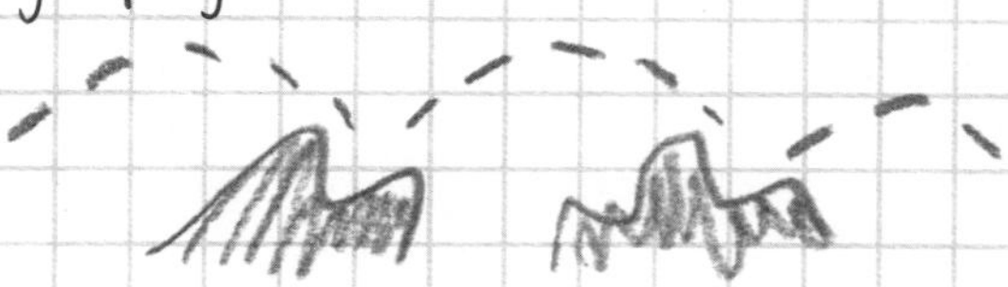

WARNING! Individual shadow smashers are silent. But put 'em together, and they

TROY CUMMINGS

has no tail, no wings, no fangs, no claws, and only one head. As a kid, he believed that monsters might really exist. Today, he's sure of it.

BEHAVIOR This creature loves crossword puzzles, but always gets stuck on 19-across.

HABITAT Troy Cummings lives in a nice little house that's about to get eaten by two giant trees.

DIET Neat joes. (Some people call 'em sloppy joes, but those people aren't eating carefully enough.)

EVIDENCE Few people believe that Troy Cummings is real. The only proof we have is that he supposedly wrote and illustrated The Eensy-Weensy Spider Freaks Out! and Giddy-up, Daddy!

WARNING! Keep your eyes peeled for more danger in The Notebook of Doom #4:

CHOMP OF THE MEAT-EATING VEGETABLES